Passive Income in the Crypto-currency Markets

High Income Opportunities in the Bitcoin and Cryptocurrency Markets

By Peter Drobny

quote or paraphrase any part or the content within this book without the consent of the author or copyright owner. Legal action will be pursued if this is breached.

Disclaimer Notice:

Please note the information contained within this document is for educational and entertainment purposes only. Every attempt has been made to provide accurate, up to date and reliable complete information. No warranties of any kind are expressed or implied. Readers acknowledge that the author is not engaging in the rendering of legal, financial, medical or professional advice.

By reading this document, the reader agrees that under no circumstances are we responsible for any losses, direct or indirect, which are incurred as a result of the use of information contained within this document, including, but not limited to - errors, omissions, or inaccuracies.

First Edition: February 2020

CONTENTS

INTRODUCTION

CRYPTO MINING

What is Crypto Mining?

How can you benefit from mining?

Resources

CRYPTO LENDING

What is Cryptocurrency Lending?

How can you benefit from cryptocurrency lending?

Resources

MASTERNODES AND STAKING

What are Masternodes?

What is Staking?

How can you benefit from Masternodes and Staking?

Resources

AIRDROPS, FORKS AND BUYBACKS

Air Drops

Forks

Burns and Buybacks

Resources

CONCLUSION

ABOUT STELLA FINANCIALS

Introduction

This book has been written to elaborate on ways to earn passive income from cryptocurrency investments.

As cryptocurrencies have proliferated throughout the digital sphere, now more than ever there are many opportunities to earn significant passive income beyond holding and trading cryptocurrencies.

If you are interested in more than just holding onto your tokens, and you want to see your investments grow, then keep reading. There are a few options available, so I am sure you will find one that fits your needs and matches your investing profile.

This article looks at a few ways to grow your crypto earnings from crypto mining, to coin lending as well as leveraging your current holdings to making savvy investments in the underlying infrastructure that supports the distributed networks your crypto currencies operate on. There are several less capital heavy and time-intensive ways to increase your crypto wealth.

Here you will get the information you need to understand how to grow your crypto holdings systematically.

Crypto Mining

What is Crypto Mining?

Cryptocurrency mining is a process in which cryptocurrency transactions are verified and are added through new blocks to the blockchain digital ledger. By adding such a block, new bitcoins are distributed. It is a resource-intensive process that ensures that a miner receives a reward for their efforts in the form of coins. There are various options for mining Bitcoin or other cryptocurrencies yourself: solo, pool or cloud mining. This requires special hardware that is either active with you or your mining service provider.

Bitcoins are produced by solving complex computing tasks. The data blocks have to be decrypted to generate a Bitcoin. So-called "Bitcoin miners" exist, which are high-performance computers that are designed for only one task: the solving of complex mathematical algorithms and the production of bitcoins. Bitcoin miners are even offered for rent. The problem in the matter is the cost / benefit factor. Such high-performance computers require huge amounts of energy and generate a lot of heat.

Another problem with profitable mining is that mining for bitcoins is becoming increasingly complex and the mining difficulty will continue to grow. The more computing power made available to Bitcoin Mining, the faster the difficulty grows - and therefore larger and larger calculating machines are needed to successfully mine Bitcoins.

Mining Bitcoin and other Cryptocurrencies with your own Hardware

To contribute as a miner to the production of blocks through your own efforts, you need special hardware in the form of ASIC (application-specific integrated circuit) chips. These are available in different price categories from various manufacturers, such as Bitmain, Whatsminer or Canaan. The best known ASIC miners are Antminers, such as the classic Antminer S9 or the latest generation Antminer S17+. In the past, Bitcoin mining was also possible via the processor of the PC, but given the increased difficulty, this approach is unprofitable since a few years. The expected electricity costs are significantly higher than the income. The most important components when choosing the right hardware include:

1) Price
2) Hashrate: in TH / s
3) Power consumption

Providing electricity costs per hash is the easiest way to compare providers: the higher the efficiency, the higher the profit potential and the higher the price.

Other Options for Bitcoin Mining

As an alternative to buying Bitcoin and mining with your own hardware, you can also operate cloud mining. In this case you invest in the hash power of a service provider who already has the necessary infrastructure. It is a temporary contract that you can enter into with companies like Genesis Mining, Hashshiny and others. The main advantages are the avoidance of additional costs and inconveniences within your own four walls, such as high electricity bills, downtime or unwanted heat. Caution should be exercised with hidden fees of any kind (electricity, operation, payment), which is why you should read the entire contract carefully. Cloud mining is particularly worthwhile for the provider as they install their equipment in countries with cheap electricity, such as Russia, China, Iceland and others.

Solo and Pool Mining

If you decide to buy hardware and are not necessarily interested in trading on a crypto exchange, you have to choose between solo and pool mining. While you act alone in solo mining, mining pools are associations of miners that bundle the computing power. Despite the fees charged by pools, it is worth joining them, as it often takes a long time for you as a solo miner to reach a paid block. In fact, unless you run a mining operation of industrial scale, it is highly unlikely that you will ever be rewarded with a block when mining on your own. By adding the computing power in the pool, earning a block reward is reached much faster and earnings are therefore also distributed earlier. The largest pools in the crypto world are BTC.com, AntPool, SlushPool and F2Pool. The industry-standard fee to join a mining pool is 1-4% per year.

Bitcoin Mining or Buying?

When is bitcoin mining worthwhile and when should you tend to buy digital currency? We take a closer look at the characteristics and list them in the table below.

Properties	Bitcoin Price	Electricity Costs	Fees	Computing Power
Mining Bitcoin / Cryptocurrencies	In mining, you benefit in relative terms when prices stagnate or increase slightly. You also make profits when prices rise, while the value of the hardware can drop significantly if prices fall.	With high electricity costs, mining may not be worthwhile.	There are fees in the form of hardware, maintenance and possibly other costs.	Special hardware is required to achieve sufficient computing power. Mining farms dominate the market with larger capacities.
Buying Bitcoin / Cryptocurrencies	You benefit especially when the Bitcoin price rises. This profit is higher than that of miners. There are no profits from stagnation and falling prices.	No impact	Depending on the respective trading platform, different fees may apply for trading.	An ordinary device is enough to buy coins.

Is Bitcoin Mining still worth it?

The short answer is that it depends where you mine and with which equipment. The high purchase costs of the hardware (USD 500-USD 3000 and higher) and electricity costs for the operation make bitcoin mining unprofitable in most countries.

After looking at all the options, the crucial question arises: is mining Bitcoin worthwhile? This is difficult to answer because even with professional hardware you still have many unknowns. The biggest factor lies in the evolution of the Bitcoin price. Your earnings usually develop in proportion to the price. If prices fall over an extended period of time, the value of your mining proceeds will fall accordingly. Moreover, the mining difficulty will increase the more mining devices and therefore computing power mine a cryptocurrency, which will lead to a lower reward per hash rate. You can get an approximate estimate of Bitcoin mining by using a Bitcoin mining calculator, such as the calculators you can find under www.whattomine.com or www.coinwarz.com. Simply enter the relevant information such as electricity price (net), exchange rate and the hash rate of your miner.

The most popular coins to mine are Bitcoin,

Zcash and Dash. You will see that depending on the miner you use and the electricity costs at which you can, mining can still be very profitable in 2020. We will provide more examples in the next chapter where we explain how you can benefit from mining.

How does Bitcoin Mining work?

Paying with bitcoins is anonymous. Neither the sender nor the receiver can see who paid what. The payment is executed through a transaction in the Bitcoin network. Only the transactions are recorded and all transactions of a certain period of time are combined into one block. The Bitcoin Miner then has the task of confirming each of these transactions and entering them on a list of the blockchain. The miner is rewarded with bitcoins for this work. To reward the miner, the bitcoin system currently provides that approximately 1800 new bitcoins are generated by miners every day, since one block of 12.5 bitcoins is mined every 10 minutes. This number will be reduced to 900 new bitcoins per day after the "halving" in 2020.

As soon as a block has been created and the transactions have been firmly written into the blockchain, 12.5 bitcoins will be distributed as a reward (currently around USD 116,000). However, to make bitcoin mining more difficult, but also to ensure that bitcoins are counterfeit-proof, the Bitcoin mechanism provides for a built-in difficulty.

In addition to the transactions and the digital fingerprint of the previous block, each block also contains a long random number. When calculating a block, a checksum (hash) must be calculated. The hash is thus a kind of fingerprint for a list of transactions with which it is easy to understand whether they have been manipulated or not, since the hash would then be different.

However, generating the hash has a built-in difficulty: the checksum must be less than a certain value. This limit depends on the current difficulty. The greater the difficulty, the smaller is this threshold. The difficulty in turn depends on how long it took to calculate the last 2016 blocks. This is because according to the Bitcoin algorithm, a new block is to be generated approximately every 10 minutes. If the last 2016 blocks were calculated in a shorter time, the difficulty is increased. If fewer bitcoins were generated during this time, the difficulty can also decrease again, but this rarely occurs.

What does a Bitcoin Miner do and how does it find new Bitcoins?

The Bitcoin Miner uses special software to search for a suitable hash with which the Bitcoin algorithm is accepted, i.e. corresponds to the current difficulty. For this purpose, a random number is written into a block within a fraction of a second and a new checksum is formed (hash). If the checksum was too large, a new random number is taken and a new checksum is generated. How quickly this process works with the current mining equipment is specified in hashes per second or kilo, mega or tera hashes per second:

Hash "H/s"	1 Hash per second
Kilo Hash "KH/s"	1.000 Hashes per second
Mega Hash "MH/s"	1.000.000 Hashes per second
Terra Hash "TH/s"	1.000.000.000 Hashes per second

The faster the checksum calculation is run, i.e. the more hashes can be calculated per second, the higher the chance of finding a suitable checksum. In between, the program also writes the newly received transactions to the block.

If a suitable hash value has been found, i.e. the checksum is below the required limit, the miner software sends the newly mined block to all Bitcoin servers. They check the block and if it is confirmed, the block is distributed to the entire Bitcoin network. As the first transaction, the miner can write 12.5 bitcoins into his own bitcoin wallet address in the new block. Thus, by creating the new block, 12.5 new bitcoins were mined at the same time.

The current hash rate of the entire Bitcoin network is around 6.3 exahashes / s (6,300,000,000,000,000 hashes per second). If you multiply this number by 600 seconds (= 10 minutes for a new block), you get 3,780,000,000,000,000,000 hashes. This is the number of hashes that have to be calculated on average to create a valid block.

How can you benefit from mining?

You have essentially three possibilities to benefit from mining. The first option is to mine on your own. In this case, you purchase your own ASIC miners, i.e. you acquire professional mining equipment, and start to mine on your own while joining a mining pool. This approach is only viable if you leave in a place with low electricity costs and dispose of the necessary infrastructure to keep noisy devices (70+ dB) at your place. To put it into perspective, the most competitive place to mine is in Siberia, Russia, where electricity costs of USD 0.03 / kWh are common. Electricity prices can be up to 10 times higher in Europe.

The second option is to use cloud mining services, where you purchase a certain amount of hash rate from a company which rents out their equipment to you for a specific amount of time. These companies have acquired the necessary infrastructure and are located in areas with low temperature and low electricity costs. However, there are many scams in this field but we provide several providers in the next chapter. These services are not as competitive as the third option presented below, but offer very low entry costs and can therefore be a good option when you start to mine and want to have your first mining experience. The largest cloud mining companies are Hashshiny, ViaBTC and Genesis Mining. We provide several alternatives and links in the next chapter on resources.

The most competitive solution available currently is to purchase professional equipment and provide it to a service provider which hosts your miners and charges a transparent maintenance and electricity fee.

For example, the company Cyberian Mine, based in Berlin but operating a mining hosting site in Siberia, Russia, currently offers an all-in fee of EUR 0.06 / kWh (USD 0.07 / kWh), which includes EUR 0.03 / kWh of electricity costs. Professional mining equipment can be purchased from the company directly.

As a case study, we calculate below the profitability of mining two popular cryptocurrencies, Bitcoin and Zcash. We use the latest and most efficient mining equipment available and calculate the potential proceeds and costs with the calculator on www.whattomine.com.

1) Bitcoin mining

ASIC Miner: AntMiner S17+

Alogorithm: SH-256

Hashrate: 73 TH/s

Electricity consumption: 2920 Watt

Cost of device: USD 2'019

Annual mining proceeds: USD 4'099

Annual mining costs (USD 0.07/kWh): USD 1'791
Annual profit: USD 2'308

This corresponds to a Return on Investment (ROI) achieved after 10.5 months. The potential profit on capital outlay p.a. is approximately +114%. However, it must be noted that the equipment wears out and the resale value in general will be lower than the purchase price.

2) Zcash mining

ASIC Miner: AntMiner Z11
Algorithm: Equihash
Hashrate: 135 ksol/s
Electricity consumption: 1418 Watt
Cost of device: USD 1'830
Annual mining proceeds: USD 3'169
Annual mining costs (USD 0.07/kWh): USD 870
Annual profit: USD 2'299

This corresponds to a Return on Investment (ROI) achieved after 9.5 months. The potential profit on capital outlay p.a. is approximately +126%. However, again it must be noted that the equipment wears out and the resale value in general will be lower than the purchase price.

The overall conclusion is that mining is indeed very profitable in 2020, if you have access to professional mining equipment and can benefit from low electricity costs or use the services of companies offering a competitive pricing.

Resources

<u>Mining profitability calculator:</u>
https://www.whattomine.com

<u>Cloud Mining Services Providers:</u>

1) Hashshiny

https://hashshiny.io/r/IW9050493

2) ViaBTC
https://www.viabtc.com/signup?refer=361296

3) HashFlare
https://hashflare.io/r/B7753C34

4) Genesis Mining

https://www.genesis-mining.com

<u>Mining Hosting Providers:</u>

Cyberian Mine

https://cyberianmine.de

Crypto Lending

What is Cryptocurrency Lending?

In this chapter, we explore the sprawling new business of decentralized crypto lending and why it's one of the hottest areas in the crypto space right now.

Ever since its inception in 2009, the blockchain and cryptocurrency space has brought technological innovation to the financial ecosystem. Bitcoin, the first cryptocurrency, was invented just after the 2008 financial crisis which brought the world economy down.

A decade later, the blockchain and crypto ecosystems are still bringing innovation into the financial ecosystem, with the introduction of decentralized finance and the creation of crypto credit markets. Now, long term holders of cryptocurrencies can lend out their crypto assets to others who have an immediate greater need for them. Users are compensated for lending out their assets with an interest rate. In simple words, the longer an asset is lent out, the more interest it rakes in. The main demand for crypto lending comes from margin trading, i.e. crypto traders and investors leveraging their crypto assets.

The lending of cryptocurrencies has been an interesting sector to observe over the past year as new products have proliferated in the market. Volatility has been an active contributor to lending rates, and with the spikes in volatility, lending rates on crypto exchanges have reached rate above 100% p.a. on some crypto assets. These developments create the opportune moment to explore margin lending products.

Margin Lending in Traditional Financial Markets

Margin lending has been a popular product offered by traditional banks and brokers for decades. It is a process whereby brokers lend either securities or cash to their clients for trading purposes. Lending rates offered by traditional brokers (e.g. Charles Schwab) typically vary between 5% to 10% depending on the broker and the loan value.

For brokers, lending is a very profitable business. To put it into perspective, even for Charles Schwab, one of the largest US brokers, >50% of their revenue comes from net interest income (i.e. lending interest earnings after deducting interest paid to account holders). Despite the fact that they are a broker and not a bank, only 40% of their revenue comes from asset management and trading fees.

Lending In Cryptocurrency Markets

Blockchain technology has become synonymous with the democratization of financial services. This is also true in the margin lending space as anyone is able to lend out their crypto assets and earn the rates that brokers and institutions have been enjoying for years. Platforms such as Celsius or Nexo have enabled interest revenues to be passed directly on to the retail audience at interest rates that are, in some instances, 10x what is available in the traditional market.

The development of cryptocurrency lending platforms can largely be attributed to the maturation of cryptocurrency market post 2017. The latest report by Credmark, a cryptocurrency credit bureau, highlights that the lending market has expanded to over $6.4bn in loans originated by Q3 2019. This is up from a mere few hundred million just a few years before.

In the cryptocurrency sector, the lending market mainly functions with a few significant participants, namely miners, traders, high net worth individuals, and institutions. The most significant driver of demand for loans (especially loans provided via margin lending), is from traders.

Most of the large cryptocurrency exchanges facilitate some form of margin trading on their platforms. Some exchanges such as Bitfinex and Poloniex, however, enable peer to peer lending using a matching engine to bring liquidity providers and traders together. Exchange lending volumes are growing as traders seeking quick, affordable liquidity options and lenders look for attractive returns.

Types of Crypto lending

Broadly speaking, crypto lending is done through two main avenues—custodial and non-custodial.

Custodial lending is a more centralized form as it involves securing a loan through a trusted third party, for example a brokerage. Custodial lending gives more power to the third party as they virtually hold complete control over a user's assets as well as sets the interest rates, and acts as a counterparty in every transaction.

Historically, custodial lending has mainly involved Bitcoin and mainly caters to institutional investors. For example, Genesis Capital, an affiliate of Genesis Trading, originated $1 billion in crypto secured loans in 2018, according to their Q4 lending snapshot. But there are new platforms like Celcius Network which offers services to retail clients as well.

The second type of crypto secured lending is the non-custodial type and it's a more decentralized form that mainly caters to traders and retail investors. This type of lending is mainly fueled by an evolving class of decentralized applications built on Ethereum. By leveraging smart contracts, these platforms can create a system where users don't have to place their trust in a centralized authority. The smart contracts have custody of the collateral over the entire loan lifecycle and are automatically repaid once the loan is repaid.

A quick look at the loans that originated since the beginning of 2019 reveals just how popular these crypto lending platforms have become. As much as $400 million loans have originated with as much as 80% of the loans originating on DAI stablecoin. It's very evident that crypto lending has gained enormous momentum in 2019.

The cryptocurrency lending market is incredibly big, but has a lot of potential for financial growth. Compound, Dharma, BlockFi, Nexo, Maker, and Nuo all present extremely powerful products in the lending space that span a variety of use cases — from small margin loans for Dapps to entire line-of-credit solutions that bridge the gap between fiat and electronic trading. Altogether, the market has huge promise for innovation and profit — restructuring the way that we interact with cryptocurrency, fiat, and the intersection of them.

How can you benefit from cryptocurrency lending?

We provide below an overview of the top crypto lending platforms currently on the market and which you can use to earn passive income. In the next chapter, Resources, we provide the relevant links to access these providers and benefit from attractive lending rates. In order to always benefit from the best rates available, you can compare rates on https://earncryptointerest.com.

Celsius network (custodial)

The celsius network is a crypto lending platform that aims to provide financial services to the unbanked. It's got an intuitive mobile app that lets you earn interest on stablecoins and a whole host of cryptocurrencies from Bitcoin to Ethereum. The Celsius network shares up to 80% of its entire income with its community members with no minimum balance, withdrawal period, and lock-up period. It offers as much as 10% interest on the top stablecoins.

Blockfi (custodial)

Blockfi likes to describe itself as a digital wealth management platform. Blockfi enables its users to earn interest on BTC, ETH, and GUSD up to 8.6% interest, compounded on a monthly basis.

Nexo (custodial)

Nexo is an instant lending platform with military-grade security (256 bit encryption). Nexo allows you to earn up to 8% interest per year with the added flexibility of withdrawing and adding funds at any time. Notably, Nexo is also secured by a USD 100 million insurance of Bitgo custodian and Lloyd's.

Compound Finance (Non-custodial, decentralized money market protocol)

Compound is essentially an algorithmic protocol that facilitates peer-to-peer (P2P) lending on the Ethereum blockchain without taking too much custody in user funds. It basically takes in funds invested by lenders and loans them out to borrowers, balancing the finances algorithmically so that the funds are never centralized in one deposit, account or wallet. It also algorithmically sets interest rates based on supply and demand. Because of the P2P and algorithmic nature, it mainly targets small margin loans, but offers fairly high efficiency. Compound's main vehicle for profits is by taking a small margin on the money it makes from loans and through its API suite.

Dharma Lever (Non-custodial, P2P lending)

Dharma lets you earn up to 7.5% on their wallet. Currently, Dharma is in the process of building its version 2.0 that will be able to interact with the Compound protocol. Interestingly, since it's a P2P lending platform the way you lend is by creating a lending offer on its platform.

Coinlend

Coinlend is a lending bot available for lending on the Bitfinex, Poloniex and Liquid exchange. Coinlend's technology optimizes the lending process by having its bot facilitating the lending of funds at optimal interest rates, based on an algorithm developed by the company, with constant monitoring of the digital asset marketplace.

This results in increased returns and less time spent monitoring lending accounts. Since its launch in May 2017, Coinlend's bots have facilitated the generation of over USD $20,000,000 for 15,000 users. Coinlend generates more than 180,000 loans daily.

	Compound	Dharma	BlockFi	nexo		nuo
product	efficient high-liquidity, small-margin loans	fixed-interest, fixed-time small-margin loans	fiat loans collateralized by crypto	line-of-credit collateralized by crypto	stablecoin lending	decentralized debt market for crypto
market	small-margin borrowers, dapps	fixed-interest & fixed-time borrowers, dapps	fiat borrowers hodling crypto	fiat customers hodling crypto	stability-focused borrowers	variety of crypto borrowers
rates	6-13%, 1.5x collateral	2-14%, 1.5x collateral	6.2%, 1.5x collateral	6.5%, 1.5x collateral	1.5x collateral	2-14%, 1.5 collateral
structure	decentralized	centralized	centralized	centralized	decentralized	decentralized
liquidity	high	average	low	low for lenders, high for borrowers	High	High

Image Credits: Paul Veradittakit

Resources

An overview of the largest players

1) Celsius Network

https://celsius.network

2) Block Fi

https://blockfi.com

3) Nexo

https://nexo.io

4) Compound Finance

https://compound.finance

5) Dharma

https://www.dharma.io

6) Coinlend

https://www.coinlend.org

A great resource to find the most competitive lending rates in the market:

https://earncryptointerest.com

Masternodes and Staking

What are Masternodes?

Taking into account current market conditions, many crypto investors are expecting further significant gains over the next years, but more and more crypto enthusiasts are gaining interest in being rewarded for holding coins. Traditional Proof-of-Work (PoW) mining as shown in chapter 1 is just one way of earning passive income with cryptocurrencies. Its profitability varies depending on various factors discussed and should therefore be complemented with additional sources such as Masternodes or Staking. Another important fact is that you do not have to be a trading guru to start gaining additional income. These are just a few reasons why more buzz has been around the Proof-of-Stake (PoS) and Masternodes (MN). Certainly they are eye-catching nowadays, and considered as the future of cryptocurrency as they use less resources compared to Proof-of-Work (PoW) mining.

Now what is a Masternode? In a nutshell, a masternode is a server on a decentralized network. Some blockchain protocols provide for the creation of particular nodes that perform additional work on the verification of transactions and bring their owners regular profits. Such nodes are called masternodes. They regularly get rewards for completing such actions.

Why do you need to launch a Masternode now, before it's too late?

Masternode is a good option to generate passive income, and there are several reasons why it might be the right time to start running a masternode or a few at once.

First of all, masternodes are not so famous for now. However, this is likely to change soon. The same applies to rewards, which could decrease every year. Secondly, the coins are cheaper than in 2017/2018, which means that the entry point at the moment is much more attractive. Finally, it's better to hold the coins and get rewards than merely hope for prices to go up.

Although according to the CoinGecko 2018 report the numbers of both masternodes and masternode coins increased significantly during the past years, there is still a substantial drop in overall value. The total market cap for masternodes coins dropped from over $12 billion in January 2018 to just over $860 million in January 2020 — a double-digit drop quarter-on-quarter.

What is the average Masternode Return on Investment (ROI)?

The best resources to track the Masternodes ROI in real-time are listed below:

1. <u>Masternodes.Pro</u> tracks all the masternode coins available in the market and provides statistics, information, price, annual return on investment, and more information about each currency.

2. <u>Masternodes.Online</u> is another website that displays the essential information about crypto masternodes.

3. Masternode.Buzz shows you the stats per week, month, and year to date. It allows to easily track recent changes.

How to select a high ROI Masternode?

We summarize a few criteria we would pay attention before investing funds in launching the masternode. First of all, it is crucial to assess the project's lifetime and the technological aspect. Make sure to ask yourself: Is there a solid roadmap? Is the company active, progressing and achieving new milestones? How undervalued the project is and what problem does it aims to solve? How strong is the team?
Pay attention to the liquidity of the coin — check out where you can trade the token, and what the daily volume is. Listing on Binance is not obligated, but it is desirable that you can trade it on several exchanges, ideally not on cxchanges with very low trading volumes. An exception can be made for new coins, which did not manage to create a buzz around themselves, attract the attention and gather a community, but have great technological potential. Although the funds invested in the launch of the masternode are under your complete control, the masternode set up process itself requires the investment of specific technical efforts and time. All these factors give a clear understanding that a

masternode launch isn't a one-click deal. We dedicate a separate section in this chapter to show how a masternode can be set up. Do not confuse investment in a masternode with trading — such an investment should be seen as a long or at least a mid-term investment.

A minimum number of coins are required to launch a masternode. This is an individual parameter for each project. Plus, it depends on your financial conditions and the amount you are ready to risk. Nevertheless, I would like to note that every coin has a different minimum amount of coins and therefore minimum dollar value to launch the masternode. The minimum amount is listed for each coin in the links provided above. At the same time, the maximum level is usually not limited.

In order to calculate the ROI, we take the percentage ratio of the expected annual profit to the number of coins that are technically necessary for launching the masternodes. The ROI is determined only by the technical parameters of the coin and active masternodes in the network itself.

Top Masternodes for Passive Income

In a later section, we will provide a way to benefit from a novel investment opportunity via professionally managed masternodes portfolios.

However, we first provide below an overview of the crypto projects which offer masternodes investments.

1. <u>Dash (Required 1,000 DASH, approx. USD 123k)</u>
A revolutionary digital money system for instant, private online or in-store payments using their secure open-source platform hosted by thousands of users around the world.

2. <u>SysCoin (Required 100,000 SYS, approx. USD 2.7k)</u>
A powerful multi-purpose platform that puts businesses on the blockchain.

3. <u>PIVX (Required 10,000 PIVX, approx. USD 2.8k)</u>
Private, instant, verified transactions. Fast, decentralized, anonymous, proof of stake cryptocurrency.

4. <u>Horizen (Required 42 ZEN (USD 0.5k) for Securenode and 500 ZEN for Supernode or USD 5.7k)</u>

Horizen is a privacy-oriented cryptocurrency and a leading-edge technology platform.

5. <u>Zcoin (Required 1,000 XZC, approx. USD 8.5k)</u>

Private financial transactions, enabled by the Zerocoin Protocol

<u>6. Energi (Required 10,000 NRG, approx. USD 17.6k)</u>
Energi aims to become a dominant cryptocurrency platform.

As setting up a masternode requires technical knowledge, guides are provided by each coin on their respective websites. However, for those who do not want to set up masternodes themselves and do not want to invest a high USD amount in a single masternode, we will provide an idea of how you can still benefit from investing in masternodes via a pooled investment, taking advantage from diversification while delegating the technicals to experts.

What is Staking?

Staking is the process of holding funds in a

cryptocurrency wallet to support the operations of a blockchain network. Essentially, you are locking cryptocurrencies to get rewards. In most cases, the process is based on users participating in blockchain activities through a personal crypto wallet.

How does staking work? As mentioned earlier, staking is the process of holding funds in order to receive rewards while at the same time contributing to the operations of a blockchain. As such, staking is widespread in networks that adopt the Proof of Stake (PoS) consensus mechanism or one of its variants.

In contrast to Proof of Work (PoW) blockchains, which rely on mining to verify and validate new blocks, PoS chains produce and validate new blocks through staking. This enables the production of blocks without the use of mining hardware (ASICs). Instead of competing for the next block with great computational effort, the PoS validators are selected according to the number of coins that they use.

Typically, users who use larger amounts of coins have a higher chance of being selected as the next block validator. While ASIC mining requires a significant investment in hardware, staking requires a direct investment (and commitment) in the cryptocurrency. Each PoS blockchain has its own staking currency.

The production of blocks by means of staking enables greater scalability. This is one of the reasons why the Ethereum network will eventually migrate from PoW to PoS during the Ethereum Casper Upgrade.

Some chains adopt the Delegated Proof of Staking (DPoS) model. It enables users to easily signal their support through other participants in the network. In other words, a trusted participant works on behalf of users in decision-making processes.

The delegated validator (nodes) are the ones that take over the most important operations and the entire management of a blockchain network. They participate in the processes for reaching consensus and defining the most important governance parameters.

Network Inflation

For some networks, staking rewards are determined as a fixed percentage "inflation rate". This encourages individuals to use their coins. This process pays off the network's operating costs for all token holders.

For example, the Stellar coin distributes its inflation

weekly to users who stack their coins in a staking pool. An advantage of this approach is that the network can pay a fixed or controlled interest rate.

For example, if a user retains 10,000 XLM for a year

and indicates an inflation target by signing a transaction on-chain, they should expect to receive 100 XLM in rewards. This would happen in the course of a year with a balanced inflation rate of 1% (without taking compounding effects into account).

The information can also be displayed to all network users who decide whether to stake or not. This could attract new stakers as it offers a predictable reward plan rather than just a likely chance of a block reward.

Staking Pool

A staking pool is created when multiple coin holders pool their resources to increase their chances of validating blocks and receiving rewards. They combine their staking power and share the possible block rewards in proportion to their individual contributions.

Pools are most effective in networks where the barrier to entry, whether technical or financial, is

relatively high. Pools often require significant setup, development, and maintenance. As a result, many pool providers charge a fee as a percentage of the staking rewards that are distributed to participants.

In addition, pools can offer additional flexibility in terms of payout times, release times and minimum credit on the network. In this way, new users are encouraged to participate, which leads to a greater decentralization of the network.

Staking Coins

Out of a total cryptocurrencies market capitalization of USD 256 billion, the market capitalization of staking coins is approximately USD 14.3 billion.

The main staking coins include Stellar (XLM), Algorand (ALGO), NEO (GAS), Ontology (ONG), VeChain (VTHO), Tron (BTT), Komodo (KMD), Stratis (STRAT), and Qtum (QTUM). A full overview can be found under www.stakingrewards.com.

In a later chapter we will show how you can benefit from staking rewards.

How can you benefit from Masternodes and Staking?

Masternodes

As mentioned in the previous chapters, Masternodes investments require extensive technical knowledge and in many cases a high minimum USD amounts to invest in one single masternode. One possibility is to invest in masternode pools, which against a fee run the masternode and pool investments of many different investors.

A great alternative is to invest in a managed masternode pool, where a team of experts follows the market constantly, identifies the right masternodes to invest in and manages all technical tasks of setting up the masternodes.

The largest provider is the company Get Node, which is the first professional masternode pool. Investments start at EUR 1'000 or 0.2 BTC, with a dashboard providing full transparency on investments and earnings. The possibility exists to transfer out 100% of the earnings, or to reinvest some of the earnings. We provide the relevant link in the Resources chapter.

Staking

Staking can be achieved in two ways, either through holding the relevant staking coins in crypto wallets offering this services, or via exchanges providing staking rewards.

The full overview of the providers is available under www.stakingrewards.com.

Among the exchanges, Binance is attractive as they do not charge any staking fee. However, they support staking for 6 coins only. However, these provide currently staking rewards of 2-11% p.a.

Among the wallets, HashQuark is the prominent provide with up to 15 coins available for staking, offering rewards up to 14% p.a..

Resources

<u>Masternodes</u>

<u>1. Masternodes.Online</u> is a website providing comprehensive, up-to-date and essential information about all crypto masternodes: https://masternodes.online

<u>2. GetNode</u> is the only professional provider of a managed masternode pool:

https://club.getnode.io/?r=F991y9634&goto=getnode
web

<u>Staking</u>

1. <u>StakingRewards.com</u> is a website providing comprehensive, up-to-date and essential information about all staking coins, as well as a list of all wallets and exchanges supporting staking:
https://www.stakingrewards.com

2. <u>Binance</u> provides staking rewards for 6 coins and charges no fee at all:
https://www.binance.com/en/register?ref=LHWF393T

3. <u>HashQuark</u> is the wallet with the largest amount of staking coins available:
https://www.hashquark.io

Airdrops, Forks and Buybacks

Taking advantage of airdrops, forks, burns, and buybacks are one of the most passive ways to earn on your investments.

While there are some real perks that come from these opportunities, they require a bit more luck from the investor than real know-how. However, you can increase the odds of benefiting from these. To do so you definitely need to follow the activity in the crypto world and watch your coins. If you get wind of an airdrop it is a good way to increase earnings in a very short period of time.

If you are willing to do some homework, this is an easy way to profit from being in the right place at the right time. In general, projects that are building apps on the protocol level are more prone to offering airdrops. As this is the case, you'll find more airdrops coming out of protocol-level cryptocurrencies like Ethereum, EOS, and Stellar.

What exactly are all of these? And how can you take advantage of these opportunities?

Air Drops

An airdrop is a widespread distribution of a cryptocurrency token or coin, which typically offers current holders of the currency a windfall straight into their wallet. These are primarily used to gain attention and new followers. The amount one can potentially receive is typically directly proportional to one's current holdings.

But if you get wind of the drop ahead of time you may have a chance to benefit from the drop. This is part of the point of an airdrop, i.e. to get the attention and to encourage others to adopt a new token. These acquisitions come for free, so long as you already hold the currency.

However, airdrops are not something you can rely on regularly to increase your earnings.

Bitcoin Cash, which is a fork off of the original Bitcoin blockchain, held one of the most noteworthy airdrops of all time. This occurred in August 2017 and resulted in the owners of the original Bitcoins owning the same sum in both Bitcoins and Bitcoin Cash. Both have lasted and Bitcoin Cash is one of the most traded currencies on exchanges.

Forks

Using a hard fork is a relatively simple tactic for investors. It is only necessary to hold the relevant coins on the day of the hard fork (usually determined by the block height). If there are two or more competing chains after the fork, the keeper has a token balance for each chain.

While these can be lucrative, forks are also a much less reliable way to earn passive income than coin-lending or other methods described in this book. Again, forks are great when they work in your favor, but you cannot count on them as a stable way to passively grow an investment portfolio.

Burns and Buybacks

Burns and buybacks, like airdrops, are variable. Burns and buybacks can sometimes mean that the creator of a cryptocurrency buys back their native token.

Buybacks are often organized in order to burn some

of the currency. This is when a company collects a certain amount of its currency. The creators then send this currency to an address with no private key, which means that no one can access the currency. It is metaphorically referred to as "burning" as the currency is eliminated artificially in an effort to control inflation.

Burning is done to create scarcity, as it eliminates some of the currency in circulation in an effort to increase the value of the remaining currency. This can be a successful move, as it eliminates the problems of over-circulation and deflation. And overall, the value of the cryptocurrency you hold should increase.

Again, you will need to hold the cryptocurrency in your own personal or cold-storage wallet to be the full recipient of the advantage of forks and airdrops. If your funds are held on an exchange, the exchange itself will likely get the funds instead. Therefore, be sure to read the fine print.

In order to take advantage of these opportunities, you have to stay on top of news on your crypto holdings, as well as following the overall crypto space in order not to miss any significant events from which you could benefit.

Resources

<u>Airdrops</u> – a great source to be on top of all pending airdrops:
https://www.airdropbob.com

<u>Coindesk</u> – one of the main crypto news website which will report the most important forks, burns and other major events:
https://www.coindesk.com

Conclusion

We have looked at multiple ways to earn passive income in the crypto space. Crypto mining can be highly profitable if the right equipment is acquired and the investor can benefit from favorable mining conditions (i.e. cheap electricity and low temperatures). Crypto lending is simple to set up and should be taken advantage of to monetize existing cryptocurrency holdings. While staking is easily accessible via wallets or exchanges and offers yields significantly higher than currently available in traditional financial markets, masternodes are even more lucrative in terms of yields but are more difficult to access. However, for each of the options we have provided viable solutions in order to make sure that you can benefit from each opportunity.

Finally, your earnings will depend on what you are willing and able to invest, which methods and coins you choose, and your trading knowledge. The actual earnings you can achieve depend on a confluence of factors. Therefore, strong predictions about what the actual earnings potential is are difficult to provide. While mining earnings can be upwards of 100% p.a. currently as shown in the example, these can evaporate fast if prices drop and the mining difficulty increases. Yields to be earned on cryptocurrency lending, staking and masternodes are more stable in the 5-15% p.a. range, but total returns can vary depending on the price evolution of the underlying coins.

One of the major factors to successfully earning passive income will be on how well you stay informed and remain calm given the bouts of volatility of the crypto market. But clearly, the crypto market offers great opportunities in 2020 as well. Most importantly, in order to reap great rewards, you will need to play the game and be invested.

About Stella Financials

Stella Financials is dedicated to provide personal finance education to each and every one. Topics cover entrepreneurship, the economy, management, business, finance and investments, your career and personal development, and new frontiers in the world of finance and business.